CIDER VINEGAR

W9-CHA-396

Cider Vinegar

*Nature's Great Health-Promoter
and Safest Treatment of Obesity*

by Cyril Scott

ATHENE PUBLISHING CO. LTD.
Wellingborough, Northamptonshire

First published 1948
Sixth edition, completely revised,
enlarged and reset,
January 1968
Second Impression January 1969
Third Impression May 1970
Fourth Impression November 1970
Fifth Impression May 1972
Sixth (revised and reset) Impression
October 1973
Seventh Impression July 1974
Eighth Impression March 1975

ISBN 0 7225 0240 0

*Made and Printed in Great Britain by
Weatherby Woolnough Ltd., Wellingborough
Northants, England.*

CONTENTS

PREFACE TO THE SIXTH EDITION

It is, generally speaking, safe to say that obesity is a condition which has somewhat puzzled the medical profession for many years; for although numerous theories about it exist, they do not entirely solve the whole problem. The simple explanation that corpulence is merely due to overeating does not cover all the facts. If greed were the sole cause of it, how can one account for the well-known case of Daniel Lambert, who was only a moderate eater and drank nothing but water, yet his enormous weight amounted to 52 stone, 11 pounds? Granted I am here citing a very extreme case; but there have been less extreme ones which are correspondingly inexplicable — not to overlook the fact that living today are thousands of grossly overweight people of both sexes, despite their being very small eaters.

In this connection the maxim holds good that whereas there may be many truths about this or that, there are certain puzzling things for which the real truth can only be ascertained when several branches of knowledge are brought into alignment. This book is concerned with one of those branches.

To state the circumstances: several decades ago, a few impressive articles appeared in *The Medical World* of U.S.A. by a leading authority on Vermont folk medicine, in which he drew attention to the highly valuable properties contained in cider vinegar; a fact generally unknown or ignored, save by the votaries of this folk medicine, as practised for some three hundred years and evolved by the trial and error method until it and its achievements might be more widely recognized, was the reason which prompted me to present the evidence with its resultant benefits, in the following pages.

January, 1968.   CYRIL SCOTT

PREFACE TO THE FIFTH EDITION

Although it has hitherto been my policy and my pleasure to mention by name the authorities for those facts or opinions alluded to in all my books, I have reluctantly been obliged, with very few exceptions, to discontinue that practice where still living individuals are concerned. My reason for so doing is that some persons have thoughtlessly caused them much annoyance by writing to them either asking questions or for further details. In thus altering my policy I wish sincerely to state that no slight whatever is intended on their names, opinions or achievements.

THE VALUABLE ELEMENTS IN APPLES

Phosphorus, chlorine, potassium, sodium, magnesium, calcium, sulphur, iron, fluorine, silicon, plus many trace minerals. These are not lost in cider vinegar.

WARNING

I must warn the reader that unless genuine cider vinegar made from proper selected cider apples as distinct from apple vinegar made with eating, cooking or mixed crop apples, is used for the remedial purposes mentioned in this book, the hoped-for results may prove disappointing. Moreover the genuine cider vinegar must be taken according to the directions. (As I have no financial interest in cider vinegar, this warning is entirely unbiassed.)

CYRIL SCOTT

THE NATURE OF CIDER VINEGAR

First, it may be asked why this particular fluid should be so beneficial? And the simple answer is that it is derived from apples, which are said to be among the most healthgiving fruits on earth. The old saying: 'an apple a day keeps the doctor away' is no empty slogan; for apples contain some very important tissue-salts, including potassium, the element of outstanding importance by which the late Dr Forbes Ross, even at the beginning of this century, successfully cured cancer.

A second question might run: what are the functions of cider vinegar — or — in layman's parlance, exactly what does it do? Stated for the moment in brief, to be enlarged upon later, it does a variety of things in an effective and *safe* manner, and though not a universal panacea, (what *is*?) nevertheless it may be rightly regarded as a proven polychrest of considerable range ... I have said *proven*: for the reader is reminded that real proof of a treatment is in its curing; a truth which has relatively been borne out by the many unsolicited letters received over the years since my (therapeutical) books were first published, i.e., letters telling me of the marked improvement in health as a result of putting into practice the information contained in them.

Having mentioned the latter few incidental facts, it now remains to state that the generally advocated proportions of the beverage are the same as given in the following section on obesity.

If, however, the *cider vinegar and honey combination treatment* be advantageously substituted, (see page 38) then the proportions of one to the other would vary according to individual taste.

The vinegar itself can, of course, be beneficially used in salads, in making mayonnaise, for pickling, indeed in substituting for ordinary vinegar in any recipe of which the latter is an ingredient.

OBESITY

As so many women are assailed with the fear of getting fat, I will deal with this condition first, though it is not looked upon as a disease in the ordinary use of the word. All the same, as the tendency to put on too much flesh occurs with either sex, it shows that 'something is wrong somewhere' though exactly what, orthodox medicos seem unable to state. When excessive corpulence is exhibited in the case of young persons, it is often attributed to defective action of some of the endocrine glands: and this may be correct. The assumption may also prove correct in the case of much older persons; but why the action of these glands is defective we are not told. That obesity often eventuates from the habit of imbibing too many alcoholic liquors, most of us have observed, but in that case the reason is obviously that the tissues get full of fluid, as the bloated appearance of the face suggests. Further there are certain drugs which are apt to cause obesity, and it has been noticed that persons who for some reason have been taking mercury or arsenic over a long period tend to increase in bulk. But leaving aside such obvious causes as over-eating, a sedentary life, and a lack of fresh air, as also the over-consumption of starchy and sugary foods, the prime cause of obesity is the insufficient oxidation of the blood. Not realizing this fact, women (in particular) will often resort to slimming measures and advertised slimming drugs which may prove very harmful in the end. Now the safe and salubrious treatment, proved over years of trial, is to be found in nothing more complicated than cider vinegar; the reason being, as already implied, that the aliment is conductive to the proper oxidation of the blood.

The *modus operandi* is as follows: two teaspoonfuls of the cider vinegar in a tumbler of water to be taken on rising in the morning. To get the desired effect, the practice is to be continued over a long period. Obesity cannot be expected to vanish in twenty-four hours! nor is it desirable that it should, as the skin requires ample time to re-adjust itself.

In severe cases cider vinegar can be taken as above indicated with the chief meals of the day, as well as in the morning. The beverage should be sipped so that the whole contents of the glass have been exhausted when the meal is finished. This, in addition to its other effects, modifies the desire to over-eat, and also promotes digestion.

Unless the effect of the treatment is spoilt through eating many starchy foods, and (this is very important) *a lot of salty foods and much salt in any form*, according to numerous reports received, the average reduction of weight resulting from taking cider vinegar is 1½ lb. a week. This usually continues until the over-stout person reaches the weight which would be right and healthy for his or her type of body. Thereafter, one glass daily of the diluted cider vinegar should serve to prevent a recurrence of the trouble, and also be beneficial for the health in general.

The following case is of interest:

Lady much too stout. Also suffering from a complaint which necessitated her having to relieve her bladder at very frequent intervals. The cider vinegar treatment got rid of her surplus fat in a matter of weeks and at the same time cured her bladder trouble.

Cider vinegar and a hot climate:

Lady, who had to spend part of her time in India, noticed that when over there she put on far too much weight. She then found that by means of the cider vinegar treatment she could keep it down to normal.

It has been noticed that in many cases a marked reduction in weight has been effected by the cider vinegar treatment only, without any change of diet. Even so, on the authority of a noted London doctor I would stress that common salt and all salty foods should be reduced to a minimum, also spices.

And now for some general observations: if a woman who is too stout will take one teaspoonful of cider vinegar in a glass of water during meals, she will generally observe that in two months her waistline has been reduced one inch. In four months two inches, and so on. But a noteworthy fact is that reduction in bulk is by no means always associated with reduction of weight. Where comparatively young women are concerned, though the tape measure may show a loss of fat, the scales will often show an actual increase in weight; the reason being an increased deposit of calcium in the bone-framework of the body due to the improved metabolism. And that the latter *has* improved is evident from a marked decrease in dental decay. It seems needless to add that under the cider vinegar treatment, surplus fat will gradually disappear no matter *where* it is present, and whether it takes the form of a double chin or an accentuated bosom. Incidentally, a London M.D. has indicated the signs of overweight as follows: when bending down is an effort; when even a little exertion causes breathlessness for no other reason than that one is too stout; when a person finds that he or she has put on about half a stone in six months. When any of these occur, they denote surplus fat, and that the individual cannot be termed in perfect health.

Of course most of us are aware that vinegar has been used as a slimming agent for a great many years (there was a time when Byron lived on vinegar and biscuits because he was getting too stout), but what should be stressed is that ordinary vinegar must *not* be used, as it does not contain the properties of vinegar made from apples, and in the long run would certainly prove harmful. We must remember however, much as we may blink our eyes to the fact, that stoutness is really a disorder which we recognize in the domestic animal kingdom but disregard in the human unless pronounced enough to be unsightly. Therefore, being a disorder, the only safe and rational way of combating it lies in a method that is conducive to better metabolism and hence improved health. All the evidence goes to show that the cider vinegar treatment will achieve this object.

EFFECTS OF CIDER VINEGAR ON THE BLOOD

When the blood is out of order owing to a deficiency of the required mineral salts and vitamins, all kinds of diseases from boils and rheumatism to cancer may occur according to the make-up of the individual. This everyone knows who has studied even the rudiments of therapeutics. There is a condition, however, which has baffled most therapeuticians, and persons suffering from this disorder are called 'bleeders', the general verdict being that nothing can be done for them, consequently they live in dread of the most trifling accident such as the cutting of a finger or a mishap while shaving.

Now it is an impressive fact that the taking of cider vinegar in the manner already indicated, favours that clotting of the blood which fails to occur in the case of 'bleeders'. The reason is again to be found in the improved metabolism which the vinegar brings about. Exponents of that most effective therapy known as the biochemic system of medicine, maintain that the haemophilia (as it is called), occurs when there is a deficiency of phosphate of potash, phosphate of iron, and to some extent chloride of sodium in the blood. Thus cider vinegar favours the assimilation of these salts, especially if two teaspoonfuls of honey are added to the beverage. (I will deal with this later.) Meanwhile we will consider the use of cider vinegar respecting surgical operations.

CIDER VINEGAR AS A HEALING AGENT

According to the evidence now to hand; if an operation is necessary following some accident, the healing process can be greatly quickened by directing the patient to take one or more teaspoon-fuls of cider vinegar in half or a whole glass of water with each meal. This practice should be continued for two or more weeks. If desired, the patient can drink the beverage between meals instead. All the evidence goes to show the astonishing efficacy of this simple treatment.

Bleeding can be reduced to a minimum by the same expedient in the case, say, of an operation on the nose for adenoids or polypi, and at the same time all likelihood of post-operative haemorrhage can be prevented. Where patients have contrived to take the cider vinegar treatment for a whole month before the operation, it has been found that the bleeding hardly amounts to a dozen drops. (I should, however, add in parenthesis that as both adenoids and polypi indicate a lack of certain mineral salts, operations can be avoided in many cases if these are taken. Furthermore, that as the habitual taking of cider vinegar improves the metabolism of the body, operations might be less frequent ordeals than in such countries where the medical profession resorts to surgery almost on the slightest pretext.)

MENSTRUATION

The number of women who suffer during their periods is legion. If menstruation is too profuse, then the cider vinegar treatment will reduce the flow to about fifty per cent, that is to say to normality. Moreover the amount of clots will be greatly decreased. This may sound like a contradiction to what has already been stated regarding the power of cider vinegar to cause blood-coagulation; but therein lies the 'magic' of this health-giving liquid – its action normalizes abnormalities! For instance, there are certain naturopathic treatments which cause some people who are too thin to become stouter, and other people who are too stout to become thinner; and if one wonders why there should be this paradoxical action, the simple answer is that such treatments promote health and consequently normality. In the case of menstruation, I should add here that a noted M.D. advised that before normality be established, the vinegar treatment may in some cases delay the onset of menstruation for a few days. Should this occur, it is advisable to cease taking the beverage for three or four days prior to the expected menstrual date. The cider vinegar treatment can then be continued when menstruation has set in.

HAEMORRHAGES, CUTS, WOUNDS

Some folk say in colloquial parlance that cider vinegar 'dries up the blood'. This is of course an overstatement. What they really mean is that as soon as a man cuts himself while shaving or in any other way the blood clots immediately on coming into contact with the air, and there is practically no bleeding. This observation having been made years ago, in cases where wounds do not heal as quickly as they should, the following procedure is resorted to: two teaspoonfuls of cider vinegar are taken in half or a whole glass of water both at meals and between meals, making six glasses in all. A weak solution of the vinegar is also applied to the wound itself. This treatment has generally proved highly efficient.

In cases of frequent nose-bleeding due to some indeterminate cause, a drink of the vinegar beverage with each meal will soon put a stop to the trouble.

The same treatment is prescribed for any indefinite haemorrhage of a small amount, from either the respiratory or the gastro-intestinal tract, so as to prevent the liability to further haemorrhage until the cause of the bleeding has been discovered. This power to stop haemorrhage again serves to demonstrate the pronounced effect cider vinegar has on the body process. For obstinate *visible* wounds, diluted crude black molasses applied as poultices has often done wonders.

EFFECT OF CIDER VINEGAR ON THE EYES

When, with the creeping on of old age, or even earlier, many people find themselves unable to read for any length of time with comfort, or they discover that they have grown oversensitive to strong light, then in numerous such cases it has been found that the cider vinegar treatment, especially when combined with honey, (see page 38), retards the onset of these conditions or acts as a cure; the reason being that it supplies the eyes with those vital elements essential to their health, and therefore, right functioning. Even cataracts (according to biotherapists) only occur when the body is lacking in the cell-salts *fluoride of calcium, phosphate of potash* and *silica*, as also in vitamin C — though the importance of vitamins for the correct functioning of all our senses being now so generally recognized, it needs no emphasis here.

IMPAIRED HEARING

Unless due to some serious ear-trouble, the same cider vinegar treatment as for eyes has frequently proved of much benefit to persons suffering from impaired hearing, thus often sparing them the necessity of resorting to a deaf-aid.

EAR DISCHARGE (OTORRHOEA)

The method of treating ear-discharge when it occurs during one of the childhood diseases is as follows: one teaspoonful of cider vinegar in a glass of water, to be taken in the middle of the morning and again in the middle of the afternoon. Under this simple treatment the discharge disappears quickly. Apropos of which, some while ago I received a letter from a gentleman who told me that for twenty-eight years he had suffered from an aural discharge which no doctor or specialist he had consulted could cure. He then came across my booklet on cider vinegar, put the therapy into practice, and completely cured himself in a very short time and without specifically treating the ear itself at all. In orthodox medical practice it would almost seem as if doctors and specialists were oblivious of the fact that the ear is a part of the human body, and not an organ detached from the physical vehicle of consciousness! Otorrhoea can only eventuate where there is a deficiency of certain of the mineral salts. Which ones are particularly lacking can be ascertained from the colour and nature of the discharge itself. In short, once again the matter boils down to defective metabolism, and that is why the above mentioned treatment produces a speedy cure.

NOSE TREATMENT

Our chemists sell all sorts of nostrums for what we call 'a stuffy nose', yet according to the many cider vinegar therapists nothing is so effective (and so cheap) as cider vinegar used as an inhalant. In a suitable vessel the vinegar is placed so as to reach a depth of about two inches. The vessel is then placed on a stove or gas-ring until its contents begin to steam. The vapour is then inhaled. Thereafter the nasal passages will remain clear from twelve to twenty-four hours. If necessary the inhalation is repeated. The effects of this treatment are to remove the congestion, to allay the inflammation of the mucous membrane, and to kill the cold-germs. Should the vinegar inhalation be too strong to be tolerated, then a little water can be added. The cider vinegar beverage should be taken with meals, or when convenient, to speed up the cure. It has been said, I may here add, that this special kind of vinegar has an adrenalin-like effect; hence its power to stop bleeding.

In cases of frequent nose-bleeding due to some indeterminate cause, a drink of the vinegar-beverage with each meal — so it has been found — will, in a short time, put a stop to the trouble.

Also, for any indeterminate bleeding of a small amount occurring in some other part of the body, the same treatment is indicated, so as to prevent the liability to further haemorrhage until the cause of it has been ascertained.

SORE THROAT

All the evidence goes to show that sore throat, even of the streptococcus type, can be cured with astonishing rapidity — often in one day — by using cider vinegar as a gargle. The sort of drugs now in vogue usually prescribed by the orthodox profession are less speedily curative than is cider vinegar gargle. Moreover the indiscriminate use of such medicaments may have very undesirable effects, as I, personally, have seen in many cases. The cider vinegar treatment consists of adding one teaspoonful of the vinegar to a glass of water. Every hour the sufferer should gargle with one mouthful of the mixture. A second mouthful should then be taken, gargled with, and then swallowed. This procedure should be repeated every sixty minutes during waking hours, or even in the night if the patient cannot sleep. As soon as the soreness has improved, the intervals of gargling, etc., can be lengthened to two hours. When the patient is cured it is advisable to use the gargle after each meal for a few days to ensure that there will be no return of the trouble.

TICKLING COUGH

Towards the end of a cold, many people suffer from that annoying and sleep-preventing irritation we call a 'tickling cough'. In many cases neither lozenges nor other measures have any result. As to most cough-mixtures which doctors prescribe, they contain a drug to deaden the nerve, and drugs in the long run are harmful; on the other hand the cider vinegar treatment is both harmless and effective. All that is necessary is to place by the bedside a glass of water to which either one or two teaspoonfuls of the vinegar have been added, then as the tickling sensation is felt, to take a few swallows of the mixture; after which the 'tickle' will rapidly disappear, leaving the sufferer able to sleep again.

ACUTE LARYNGITIS

For this distressing condition the effect of the cider vinegar treatment is almost miraculous. The dosage is one teaspoonful of the vinegar to half a glass of water, the mixture to be taken every hour for seven hours. In most cases the sufferer will be talking normally again after the seventh dose. This treatment is also of great value as a precautionary measure when obliged to be with people suffering from the complaint.

ASTHMA

A somewhat similar treatment is very helpful in cases of that mild type of asthma which only occurs during the night, and where the wheezing interferes with sleep. One tablespoonful of cider vinegar is added to a tumbler of water, which should be taken in sips for half an hour. The patient should then wait half an hour, then the procedure should be repeated. If the wheezing should still persist, though usually it has gone by then, a second glass of the same mixture should be sipped.

Sufferers from severer forms of asthma would be well advised to consult a homoeopathic or a biochemic practitioner, since not all orthodox doctors are successful in dealing with this distressing complaint. Quite often it occurs as the result of suppressing some skin disease. The homoeopath, being aware of this fact, will therefore treat it accordingly. Very important are breathing exercises. Deep breathing should be practised gradually, and if persisted with every day, will, in combination with the cider vinegar treatment, most likely effect a cure, especially if the cause of the disorder has first been ascertained and dealt with by a competent practitioner.

THE MIND, MENTAL VIGOUR IN OLD AGE

There are two methods by which ageing humankind can combat senility and loss of mental vigour. One is the habitual taking of the cider vinegar as a beverage, the other is to take at least two glasses of cider proper every day. But unfortunately some of the cider in this country, nowadays, lacks the qualities of the finest kind, hence it is better to drink the cider vinegar beverage, which not only contains all the curative elements, but also comes much cheaper. That it has the power to retard the disabilities of old age is evidenced by the extraordinary physical and mental vigour of its consumers who have reached their eighties. Yet although this may be surprising on the surface, it becomes less so when we remember that cider vinegar favours the proper metabolism of the body. Nor is this all; for it has been found that the diluted vinegar beverage will restore mental and physical vigour in cases where it has already been lost. (I am here, of course, alluding to persons who newly resort to the treatment, and not to those who have made it a part of their daily lives.) And when I speak of mental vigour, it includes a marked improvement of the memory. Observers have been quite astonished to see how forgetfulness in old people partially or wholly disappeared after resorting to the practice of taking one teaspoonful of the cider vinegar in a whole glass of water, either with meals or between meals, whichever method is preferred or suits the individual best. I mention this because some people are apt to say that drinking with meals gives them indigestion. Precisely; if by drinking is meant gulping down large draughts of liquid. But then all liquids possessing any taste should be sipped and not imbibed in that unwise manner. If the cider vinegar is taken with meals in the prescribed manner, it will seldom cause indigestion, for the reason that it bears a closer resemblance to the gastric juices than does any other fluid.

THE DIGESTIVE TRACT

Which brings us to the subject of digestion and indigestion. Many people are aware that an apple is good for biliousness; it is also the remedy to take when nausea occurs after the smoking of a too strong cigar or pipe. Therefore it is no matter of surprise that vinegar made from apples is very helpful towards the cure of many digestive troubles if taken as already indicated.

FOOD POISONING

One of the most serious, if temporary, disturbances of the digestive tract is caused, as we all know, by food poisoning. Yet with cider vinegar therapy the method to cure these effects is quite simple. The sufferer adds one teaspoonful of cider vinegar to a glass of water, and sips one to two teaspoonfuls of the mixture every five minutes. This procedure is repeated as many times as may be necessary. The whole contents of the glass is not taken at once, because the stomach, owing to its disordered state will not tolerate it; only in small amounts can the mixture be kept down. As soon as a marked improvement takes place, then the intervals between taking the remedy are lengthened. As the result of this treatment the painful symptoms have usually vanished within twelve hours, after which the cider vinegar beverage is taken with meals for a few days to complete the cure.

THE TREATMENT FOR DIARRHOEA

Diarrhoea being an attempt on the part of nature to get rid of poisons in the body, only unenlightened physicians will seek to stop the attack by unnatural means, though if it continues too long, measures sometimes need to be taken to prevent it from over-weakening the patient. And when I say unnatural means, I refer to such drugs as calomel or laudanum, which orthodox doctors often prescribe. Even castor oil is not good, as, like laudanum, it constipates the patient afterwards. And in any case these drugs do not cure the cause of the disease but merely deal with its effects. Unless diarrhoea is due to some serious bodily disorder, it can be cured in a very short time by the cider vinegar treatment; namely one teaspoonful of the vinegar to a glass of water, to be taken not only with meals, but in addition in the middle of the morning, in the middle of the afternoon, and again at bedtime. It does not matter what age the patient happens to be; for apart from being effective, it is so harmless that it can be given to children of only three years of age. The cider vinegar treatment acts as an antiseptic to the intestines and the whole digestive tract, hence it is an entirely rational method of dealing with an abnormal condition. Not only will it cure humans but also animals; a fact that has been proved over and over again.

CIDER VINEGAR AS AN ANTISEPTIC

I have already mentioned that the cider vinegar possesses antiseptic properties, and it may be asked what proof there is for this assertion? The answer is that after taking this beverage over a given period, there is no odour either in the flatus or in the excreta; which is enough proof in itself. The reason is that the vinegar destroys the putrefactive bacteria in the digestive tract.

To enlarge on the subject: nowadays that 'a clean bowel is one of the most essential pre-requisites to good health and vigour', is a maxim the truth of which is being more and more accepted by healers of all schools. And the proof of a clean bowel is determined from the odourless-ness of both flatus and excreta. Where there is odour, it nearly always means intestinal putrefac-tion — though admittedly offensive flatus may occur after eating raw onions, owing to the sulphur which they contain. Eggs, unless entirely fresh, are apt to produce similar unpleasant effects, likewise cabbage. But we are not concerned with the purely temporary results consequent on eating these particular aliments, but with that more or less permanent state of intestinal putrefaction which makes people an offence to others and an offence to themselves! Now in this connection it is of interest to note that putrefaction and decomposition are practically synonymous words; consequently the contentions of a distinguished Australian physician are highly significant. He maintains that *decomposition* is the prime cause of all diseases, and hence that the most rational way to prevent and cure human ills is to be found in some agent which prevents decomposition. He advocates phosphorus (though obviously in minute doses) treated in a certain way by sunlight; but as this would be dangerous to take without a doctor's advice (one man killed himself with an overdose) the cider vinegar treatment is safer. Moreover, applies do contain phosphorus, and be it noted in a more natural and safer form.

AUTO-INTOXICATION

From the foregoing it will be inferred, and rightly so, that cider vinegar is the preventive *par excellence* of auto-intoxication, from which so many people suffer in varying degrees. One reason why the vinegar prevents this disease-promoting condition is to be found in its action on the liver, for it has the power of detoxicating the poisons that accumulate in the organ, and at the same time implementing their elimination from the body.

Cider vinegar may therefore aptly be called an hepatic remedy, and one namely which possesses none of those disadvantages present in many drugs which people are in the habit of taking for what they are wont to term 'a touch of liver'. For proper elimination, a substance called pectin is necessary, as it has the power to draw water to itself; to cause a swelling of foods 'responsible for the bulk in the intestine'; it is moreover a binding, jellifying and hence a thickening agent. As pectin is an ingredient in cider vinegar, to the former may be ascribed its capacity to promote adequate and healthy action of the bowels, similar to that produced by taking linseed (whole) last thing at night with a little water. The linseeds swell and to some extent jellify, and thus produce the desired effect. But that is merely by the way; the linseed treatment will in most cases not be required if the cider vinegar beverage is taken. Nowadays we hear of the necessity of creating 'bulk' in the intestines, but as this necessitates the eating of more than it may be advisable to consume, the cider vinegar treatment is to be preferred, seeing that it enables the appetite to be satisfied with a lesser amount of food.

ERUCTATIONS, HEARTBURN, BAD TASTE, HICCOUGHS

Unless due to some serious disorder of the stomach, or to the habit of swallowing air, eructations can be cured or greatly lessened by taking the cider vinegar beverage with the chief meals of the day.

As for heartburn, that burning sensation which

may occur after meals — sometimes one or two hours after — this often disappears entirely after resorting to the cider vinegar beverage, or at any rate it is much lessened.

When a bad taste in the mouth is noticed on rising in the morning, one teaspoonful of the vinegar to a glassful of water if used as a mouth-wash will quickly dispel it.

Hiccoughs, when not due to some serious condition, can be relieved at once by taking one teaspoonful of cider vinegar — *neat* — so says an eminent M.D.

EFFECT OF CIDER VINEGAR ON THE URINE

If the urine is either too acid or too alkaline, that troublesome and embarrassing necessity for much too frequent urination occurs in both sexes. We are of course not here concerned with serious disorders of the urinary tract, which need special treatment, but with conditions in which the urine for no very grave reason is of an abnormal consistency. In the case of younger people it is often a too alkaline urine that necessitates frequent micturation, whereas in older people the cause may be found in the fact that the urine is too acid. But whether too acid or too alkaline, it can, according to cider vinegar healing be brought back to normal if the beverage (two teaspoonfuls of vinegar to the glass of water) be taken with the chief meals of the day. Elderly men will often find this treatment very helpful in relieving the frequent desire to pass urine during the night. Strange to say, this may occur, not always from drinking too much, but from drinking too little *water*; in which case the urine becomes too concentrated and so causes an irritation which provokes the constant urge to micturate. When this happens, elderly men are apt to get apprehensive and imagine they are suffering from prostate trouble, whereas·the real cause may be nothing more serious than a too acid condition of their urine which the cider vinegar treatment will set right ... Naturally people can inadvisedly drink too much fluid instead of too little. But here again the cider beverage proves very useful, for if taken with meals it allays any sensation of thirst between mealtimes. Yet should thirst occur owing to very hot weather, it proves to be one of the best thirst-quenchers that exist. It also has the power to allay the pangs of hunger, if for some reason a meal has to be omitted. If two teaspoonfuls of honey can be added to the drink, so much the better; the combination of the two aliments has been found to be very sustaining. I shall have a few words to say about this combination later on.

TREATMENT FOR THE HAIR

At a certain time of the year it is normal for the hair to fall out when being combed, but should new hairs not grow again, and the falling-out period be unduly protracted, thus showing a pronounced thinning of the hair, it is an indication of faulty metabolism and an abnormal state which needs correction. Now repeated observation has proved that if the cider vinegar beverage is taken with or between meals (one teaspoonful to the glass of water) not only will the hair cease to fall out, but it will grow much more rapidly and more thickly, especially if one level teaspoonful of horseradish is taken with the two chief meals of the day. The desired effect will be produced in from one to two months. Falling out of the hair is primarily due to deficiency of the tissue-salts chloride of sodium (in minute doses), phosphate of calcium, and silica; sulphate of calcium may also be lacking in some cases. Thus the cider vinegar, through its remarkable properties, re-establishes the balance, supplies the deficiencies, and so effects a cure, if persisted in long enough. It is even advisable to continue the cider vinegar treatment almost indefinitely to ensure that there be no recurrence of the trouble.

THE FINGER NAILS

When the nails become too thin or fragile and tear, bend, peel, or break; in short, when they are not of normal thickness and strength, that is again a sign of faulty metabolism, which the cider vinegar treatment will remedy. Persons with defective nails have noticed that after taking the vinegar beverage over a certain time for the purpose of curing some ailment, their nails have automatically undergone a decided change for the better, in fact they have become healthy and normal again. Furthermore, if any white spots had been present, these have disappeared. All of which points to the effects of the cider vinegar on the mineral metabolism of the body.

THE TEETH, SORE MOUTH

I have already been able to draw attention to the beneficial effects of the cider vinegar beverage on the teeth; this as briefly stated before, being due to the improved calcium metabolism which the vinegar brings about. But local measures are also indicated to prevent decay, and particularly to get rid of tartar deposit, or to prevent it from forming. For this purpose one teaspoonful of the cider vinegar should be added to a glass of water for a mouth-wash, which should be used night and morning. The teeth should also be brushed with the solution. By this simple procedure the teeth will be whitened and be much less liable to decay. I may add that the whiteness of cider vinegar drinkers' teeth is a striking proof of the efficacy of this combined treatment of taking the beverage as a habit and of using the solution as a dentifrice. Incidentally, the lime deposit in a kettle can be easily removed by adding two tablespoonfuls of the vinegar to the kettle of water, then leaving it for a time, after which the lime will come away when the water is poured out of the vessel: or it can the more easily be scraped away without injuring the interior surface.

For 'canker sores' in the mouth, the cider vinegar therapeutists prescribe the same solution as for the preservation of the teeth; namely one teaspoonful to a glass of water, the mixture to be used frequently as a mouthwash. Under this treatment the sores will generally have vanished within twenty-four hours.

For gums that have a marked tendency to bleed, the cider vinegar beverage should be taken with meals, and the mouthwash used as indicated above.

TREATMENT FOR THE JOINTS

When the joints in any part of the body start to 'creak', the cider vinegar beverage should be taken with meals. It has generally been noticed that under this treatment the cure will be effected in about one month: though in the case of a calcium deposit in the shoulder bursa, it may take two months. 'Creaking joints' are apt to occur in elderly people, but according to many reports to hand, age as a general rule proves no obstacle to the cure. Regarded from the biochemic standpoint 'creakings' become noticeable where there is a deficiency of minute doses of sodium chloride in the system. This may seem curious, as most people eat salt (much too much of it): but then salt taken in crude doses as a condiment has a very different effect from the triturated kind. The human body can only absorb the mineral salts in the infinitesimal quantities in which nature supplies them; hence, strange though it may sound, a person can be starved of salt even when he eats a large amount of it. Too much common salt disturbs the metabolism of the body, consequently it is best to cut down its consumption to a minimum, and so give the cider vinegar treatment every facility to do its work.

VERTIGO

Dizziness may arise from various causes, some of them serious, others transient, such as a disordered stomach or liver. Heart-trouble and anaemia of the brain are often responsible for giddiness, and of course both these grave conditions require special treatment. In some cases where anaemia is present or where the heart is involved, molasses often proves most useful as a heart-muscle strengthener. (See book entitled *Crude Black Molasses*.) If molasses should be unobtainable, then black treacle is of value. Sufferers from 'heart' should always eat honey instead of jam, owing to the valuable properties that the former contains, and on which I shall enlarge later. For anaemia, molasses (or failing that, black treacle) have proved to be remarkable curative. The crude doses of iron so often prescribed by orthodox doctors are not only apt to be useless but also harmful, whereas the iron in molasses or black treacle is assimilated by the organism and hence is frequently productive of the desired result when all other treatments have failed. Even so, the cider vinegar beverage can be profitably employed to enhance the treatment. Should vertigo not be associated with serious diseases the cider vinegar taken with meals will, judging from all the evidence, bring about a cure in from four to eight weeks. One may ask if there is any hope of relief or cure in cases of Ménière's disease? To which I can only reply that there is at any rate *some* hope, for the following reason. The giddiness with this disease is usually caused by haemorrhage into the internal ear; but as we have seen from the testimony supplied, the cider vinegar treatment both prevents and cures the tendency to internal bleeding, therefore it would be fairly reasonable to infer that in some cases good results might be obtained. Indeed for all one knows, in cider vinegar therapy perhaps may be found the most rational means of combating the disorder. In any event, in view of its harmlessness, it could be tried out.

TWITCHINGS

There is an annoying if minor complaint which manifests itself in twitchings of the eyelid or corner of the mouth. This is occasionally noticeable in fairly young children. A cure may often be effected of this nervous condition by prescribing one teaspoonful of the vinegar in a glass of equal parts of grape-juice and water; the mixture to be taken in the middle of the morning and again in the middle of the afternoon.

ECZEMA, DANDRUFF

For this troublesome complaint the cider vinegar beverage should be taken with meals, and the vinegar, diluted, applied to the skin. For dandruff it should be applied to the scalp.

Eczema can occur as one of the long delayed after-effects of vaccination. In general it arises from a deficiency of chloride of potassium (*kali mur.*) in the organism, especially if it is of the fibrinous type, with mealy flour-like scales. And here it is worthy of note that *kali mur.* is one of the minerals contained in apples, hence the value of the vinegar, for this salt is not lost even though the apples forming it have undergone a transformation. The dry type of eczema is frequently the result of eating too much common salt, in which case it stands to reason that the habit should be discontinued. If people *must* take salt with their meals, then they can procure non-toxic biochemic table salt at the health food stores. As this contains all the twelve tissue salts it does not upset the chemical balance of the body. To speed up recovery, attention should be paid to diet. The treatment of eczema with suppressive ointments is a gross misdemeanour against nature, as every naturopath knows and every doctor ought to know. If poisons which are seeking a way out of the body through the skin are prevented from doing so, the result is a foregone conclusion to all persons with an ounce of intelligence. Need more be said?

PILES – AN OBSTINATE CASE

The patient suffered from this complaint for four years. Itching became unbearable – disturbed nights and slight oozing were experienced. After the first application of the cider vinegar dilution the itching subsided, followed by a good night. The treatment was repeated every night; and in three weeks the piles had completely vanished. The cider vinegar was also taken internally.

NETTLE-RASH

For this condition the cider vinegar beverage should be taken with meals until the disorder clears up. It is usually due to food poisoning resulting from eating shell-fish or the like, and as we have seen that the vinegar is a remedy for same, I need not go into further details.

EFFECTS OF SUMMER HEAT

The cider vinegar beverage counteracts the fatigue and lassitude which many people feel in hot weather.

I have now given a fairly long list of the various

complaints that yield to a treatment which is as simple as it is effective. Doubtless several more could be added to the list, but it seems unnecessary to do so if the reader will bear in mind that cider vinegar is not a specific for any given disease or diseases but a promoter of general health. This it brings about, I repeat, by its influence on the metabolism and eliminative processes of the body. When these are defective, it is noticeable from many signs to which the majority of people pay little attention, being under the impression that they are merely the unavoidable results of advancing years, and that nothing can be done about them. Yet the exponents of the healing method in question think otherwise. To sum up: they maintain that metabolism and oxidation are inadequate, and health not up to standard level when the body shows signs of growing fat whilst the hair shows signs of growing thin; when the teeth are apt to decay; when the eyes get easily tired; when hearing is impaired; when the finger nails are fragile; when the joints begin to creak, to say nothing of the onset of what are recognized as actual diseases. These manifestations need not inevitably occur, say the cider vinegar 'fans' and practitioners, if the right steps are taken to prevent them. What the first and important step consists of will have become obvious to the reader; but the therapy can be enhanced by the use of honey, which is so valuable a substance that for the benefit of those who do not appreciate the fact, I will go into some details relative to its constituents.

CIDER VINEGAR/HONEY MIXTURE

Honey is not sufficiently appreciated in this country except by naturopaths and the like, despite the fact that Russian medico-scientists have shown that it will cure such a serious condition as gastric ulcer. Many English people complain that this poetic, fragrant 'syrup of the bees' is far too sickly to suit the palate. Its· sickliness however, soon vanishes if taken mixed with the cider vinegar in the proportions to be mentioned anon. Meanwhile in order to awaken some enthusiasm for honey in the general reader, I will mention the valuable elements it contains: though admittedly these are merely of academic interest, for the proof of the value of honey lies in its effects and not in the theories involving polysyllabic words as to why it produces those effects. To begin with, it contains Vitamin B_1, called thiamine, which is to be found in the *husks* of cereal grains, and is therefore lacking in *white* bread. Secondly it contains vitamin B_2, called riboflavin, which is to be found in yeast, milk, and meat, also in fish and liver. Thirdly it contains vitamin C (ascorbic acid) to be found in fresh fruits (oranges, etc.), and in fresh greenstuffs. To complete the list, honey also contains pantothenic acid, pyridoxine and nicotinic acid, the latter being part of the B_2 complex. When there is a complete lack of B_1 in the diet, that grave disease called beri-beri ensues, but where there is a shortage but not a complete lack of the thiamine, then muscular weakness and heart weakness are frequently the result. As for Vitamin C, a complete lack of it results in scurvy, and a partial lack of it in swellings and inflammation of the gums, loss of teeth, haemorrhages under the skin, and other serious conditions. All of which point to the fact that a well-balanced diet is the prerequisite to health. But as in these years of costly living it is not always possible to maintain a well-balanced diet, much the best thing to do is to take honey, seeing that it possesses all the elements essential for physical well-being. Moreover it retains those elements indefinitely, which is more than vegetables and fruits do, as unfortunately they lose some of their vitamin content within about twenty-four hours after they have been picked. The minerals in honey are even more important than the vitamins; they comprise potassium (a preventive of growths), sodium, calcium, magnesium, iron (very important), copper (good for the liver), chlorine, manganese, sulphur (the blood purifier), and silica. As these minute quantities of minerals essential for bodily health are used up in certain of the body processes, too complex to explain here, they need constantly to be replaced; hence the value of taking honey as the most simple means of achieving this end. Nor must we forget that honey also contains enzymes as they are termed, these enzymes being present in the digestive juices and in many of the tissues, consequently they aid digestion; yet honey itself requires no process of digestion before it can be utilized by the body. Nor can micro-organisms adversely affect it, for should they come into contact with it they are quickly destroyed.

In short, honey is a perfect food; it contains no harmful chemicals (or ought not to do unless it has been tampered with) and not more than one-hundredth part of it is wastage. Truly is it a food for the gods!

Taking all this into consideration, two teaspoonfuls of honey at the least should form part of the daily diet of ailing persons who wish to get well and of all well persons who desire to maintain their health. (I word my sentence in this somewhat curious manner, because there are numerous people, especially women, who do not wish to get well, and who for purposes of self-dramatization and the urge to evoke sympathy make as it were a hobby of ill-health. And although they enjoy the attention of their doctors, they would be very disappointed if one or the other cured their complaints. For such professional invalids of course nothing can be done, and they must be left to 'dree their ane weird' as the Scotlanders say.) Needless to say honey can be eaten in place of jam, or strained honey can with advantage be added to the cider vinegar beverage, in which case it makes a very palatable drink. That eminent hydropathist, the late Father Kneipp of Germany, maintained that if a little honey were added to all herbal remedies it greatly enhanced their efficacy, as it acted as a medium to promote better assimilation. Thus, the action of the cider vinegar can be improved and speeded by the same means. In addition to all the other things it accomplishes, the cider vinegar and honey combination is in many cases most helpful in promoting sound, healthy sleep. Moreover, it is a harmless one, which cannot be said of some of the drugs taken for sleeplessness at the present time.

INSOMNIA

To combat this troublesome complaint, the following measures are advocated in cider vinegar therapeutics. According to these, an immediate improvement in the ability to sleep is brought about by taking at bedtime two teaspoonfuls of the vinegar plus two teaspoonfuls of honey in a glass of water. Another glassful of the mixture should be placed by the bedside so that it may be taken in case the sufferer should wake in the night.

Granted that the causes of insomnia may be many and varied, yet this treatment is a rational one in view of the elements which both the cider vinegar and the honey contain. The prime cause of insomnia, though orthodox physicians seem still to be unaware of the fact, is to be found in a deficiency of phosphate of potash and phosphate of iron; though in some cases there may be also a deficiency of phosphate of magnesia. We all know of course that worry prevents one from sleeping, yet worry would not and need not prove unduly harmful if the phosphate of potash (*kali phos.*), which it uses up were speedily replenished. As drug soporifics do not make good the deficiency, they do not and can not *cure* insomnia, even though they may make the sufferer sleep as long as he takes them. But as soon as he ceases to take them, he finds himself as sleepless as ever, thus proving their lack of power to effect a cure. I do not here deny their usefulness to induce sleep in cases of severe illnesses; but, then we are not here concerned with these but with insomnia as a complaint in itself. Again, despite what is said to the contrary, sleeping drugs are habit-forming, though they are sometimes useful to break a habit — namely that of not sleeping, when it is but a habit. Even so, if taken for more than a very

short time, they only break one habit and form
another. Therefore when all is said, bad sleepers
would be well advised to try the harmless and
beneficial cider vinegar and honey treatment.
Should that fail in some cases then it is advisable to
take *kali phos.* 3x for a few days, three tablets
thrice daily between meals. If sufferers notice that
they get a flushed face at night as soon as they lie
down or at other times, then *ferrum phos.* 3x or 6x
is also indicated, and it should be taken intercurrently with the *kali phos.*, the latter being
excellent in order to counteract the nervous
tension responsible for some forms of insomnia.

HAY FEVER

Why only some people — and not all those living in
the heart of the country — should be adversely
affected by pollens, is something of a mystery
except to biotherapists, who maintain with good
reason that hey fever is apt to occur when the
tissues are lacking in certain salts which normally
create a healthy resistance to these airborne
substances.

True, the cause of an allergy, even to pollens,
can be a purely psychological one. But when this is
not the cause, although the cider vinegar-cum-
honey treatment should not rightly be listed as a
direct specific for hay fever, nevertheless, seeing
that it promotes the general health of the tissues,
this fact accounts for the cases in which it has
proved curative, and hence is worthy of mention in
this book.

Significantly, it has been found that in some
cases of hay fever, repeated doses of vitamin A and

vitamin C have acted very favourably: these are the particular vitamins contained in apples, and hence in cider vinegar.

COLITIS
Same as above. (Enemata with a teaspoonful or more of molasses, very helpful.)

NEURITIS
Same as above.

ARTHRITIS
The cider vinegar and honey treatment, and also the molasses treatment. Regarding the latter, I may cite a recent case history, remarkable for the rapidity of the cure. Lady turned seventy. Complete fixation of the hip joints for three years. Knees could not be flexed. Much pain and fatigue. Injections given, but with no result. Specialist finally suggested an expensive operation, but could promise no success. Operation declined. Patient was then induced by an acquaintance to try molasses, which she contrived to obtain. After thirty-six doses she could walk without sticks and could kick her posterior with her heels. Had she then known of the cider vinegar and honey combination and could have combined the two therapies the cure might well have proved even more rapid still.

TOBACCO

Although cider vinegar antidotes tobacco, as do other vinegars (W. Boericke, M.D.), that is not to say that it counteracts the harmful effects of the paper in cigarettes.

DISEASES OF CIVILIZATION

It is well known that some primitive peoples have possessed excellent health until they adopted certain of the food and drink habits of civilization. And yet, as naturopaths and biochemists maintain and have proved, it is not only some of those unwholesome foods we habitually eat in civilized countries, but — paradoxical though it may sound — those foods we fail to eat, which cause so many of our present-day diseases; and I venture to include cancer.

Admittedly, flesh sustenance, denatured and processed fare, in other words, *refined* foods, may nourish the body and keep it alive; but more than just nourishment is required to keep it in sound health, to be conducive to longevity, and to the prevention of that undesirable condition politely referred to as overweight — a condition which has become increasingly noticeable as one walks the streets today.

Another sign that something must decidedly be wanting in our generally-assumed-to-be-civilized food habits is, of course, the enormous sale of medicaments of all varieties by which people seek to calm themselves or 'buck themselves up', induce adequate bowel actions, relieve the pains of chronic ailments, counteract sleeplessness or whatever their respective trouble happens to be. All of which goes to show that the advice to include in one's daily diet an adequate proportion of natural vital foods, at any rate as far as possible, is a rational one based on sound principles.

A NOTE OF WARNING

A few words of warning are here advisable. Naturally the cider vinegar-honey-molasses trinity cannot work absolute miracles. It stands to reason that it cannot counteract evil vices, nor can it be expected to set right such ailments as require manipulative treatment. Last century Dr Still of U.S.A. discovered that priceless boon to mankind known as osteopathy, which requires no advertising from my modest pen. All I would remind the reader of is this; that for such people who, after paying due attention to the laws of health still find themselves ailing, the services of a competent osteopath are indicated.

ANSWER TO QUESTIONERS

It may be asked: will cider vinegar suit *everybody*? And yet 'everybody' is such an all-embracing word that, as the Germans say, 'therewith is nothing to be commenced!' For instance, I had a friend for whom fish was so poisonous that even if he licked a postage stamp, on which was the formerly used fish-containing adhesive, his face swelled up to such an extent that he could not see out of his eyes till the bad effects had worn off: and this despite his being a very healthy man . . . Another instance was that of a female cousin of mine who could never take a drink of pure water without regurgitating it immediately. It seems needless to add that puzzling peculiarities are many and varied, some associated with advancing years, others not. The late doctor, Sir Arbuthnot Lane declared that most elderly people could not digest pastry — yet it is related that the poet Lord Tennyson ate apple pie every day and nevertheless lived till he was eighty-three. In any case, the word 'pastry' covers a number of different sorts. As against that, legions of persons, as we all know, can eat fish, drink water, and eat pastry without suffering any untoward results. In short, there are many things that will suit many people but there is nothing that will suit *everybody*. Nevertheless it is safe to say that persons who suffer from strange idiosyncrasies are a minority and exceptions to the general rule; and if in advocating some treatment or regime one had to take all the exceptions into account, one could never advocate any treatment at all! The point is, will it suit the majority, not will it suit every man, woman and child on the whole surface of the globe! As to cider vinegar, this, judging from what we have been told, would seem to be a natural fluid for which even young children crave. One has heard that more mothers find it necessary to hide the vinegar bottle than the sugar bowl, for if they get the chance, children will pour out the vinegar into a dish, then having dipped bread or biscuits into it, will proceed to eat them with relish. And granted that one can have too much of a good thing, this intense liking for vinegar can only be accounted for by the presence of some instinct in those children's make-up. Moreover that this instinct is a natural one will have become obvious to the reader in view of the health–

promoting elements the cider vinegar contains, as also what it accomplishes when taken as prescribed.

Finally, a word may be addressed to sceptics who might say that the cider vinegar cure for human ills is all a matter of faith; for how can anything so simple prove such a polychrest? Yet if faith were the basic cause of its efficacy, it would not work with animals ... Indeed, I think that if veterinary surgeons would consider adapting the therapy outlined in this book to some of their animal patients, they would be pleased with the results.

A FEW NOTES FOR VETS

Usually, after a cow has given birth to her calf, and retains her placenta, the discharge is profuse and the affluvia overpowering. These manifestations have not occurred, however, when the cow has been given by mouth six ounces of cider vinegar added to equal parts of water, at certain times each day as long as the placenta has been retained. Of the effects of the vinegar on cows suffering from diarrhoea or imperfect digestion I may point out that experience has shown that cows thus suffering can be cured in a very few days or less by likewise giving them to drink six ounces of cider vinegar in the same amount of water. Goats with the same complaint can be speedily cured by pouring four tablespoonfuls of the mixture over their rations at each feeding time. As for dogs, their condition will greatly improve by adding a little cider vinegar to their drinking water. If done daily as a routine measure, it will tend to keep them in excellent health.

As I believe cider vinegar to be the complement of molasses, may this sequel to my earlier brochure indirectly help my fellow humans to a state of better health, and also ease the burden of our over-worked doctors.

APPENDIX

ARTHRITIS. I have known some spectacular cures affected by means of parsley tea, made like ordinary tea but taken cold. Two cups of this taken daily at some convenient times could be taken intercurrently with the cider vinegar treatment.

HIGH BLOOD PRESSURE. The remedy (sold at some health food stores) for this affliction is 'rutin', the less expensive is cider vinegar, and the remedy that costs nothing at all save the trouble of picking them, is ordinary stinging nettles taken in the form of tea. A combination of the latter with the cider vinegar treatment is well worth considering. The two remedies to be taken intercurrently, not the one mixed with the other.